LINCOLN ON THE EVE

of '61

Lincoln

ON THE EVE OF '61

A Journalist's Story by

HENRY VILLARD

EDITED BY

Harold G. & Oswald Garrison Villard

GREENWOOD PRESS, PUBLISHERS
WESTPORT, CONNECTICUT

E457.4
V55
1974

Library of Congress Cataloging in Publication Data

Villard, Henry, 1835-1900.
    Lincoln on the eve of '61.

    1. Lincoln, Abraham, Pres. U. S., 1809-1865.
I. Title.
E457.4.V55 1973   973.7'092'4 [B]   73-16631
ISBN 0-8371-7202-0

Originally published in 1941 by Alfred A. Knopf, New York

Reprinted with the permission of Henry H. Villard and
Vincent Villard

Reprinted in 1974 by Greenwood Press,
a division of Williamhouse-Regency Inc.

Library of Congress Catalog Card Number 73-16631

ISBN 0-8371-7202-0

Printed in the United States of America

FOREWORD

In the romantic life of Henry Villard, immigrant, pioneer, journalist, Civil War correspondent and later a great figure in the railway world and the completor of the Northern Pacific Railroad, no event was more remarkable than his being stationed at Springfield after the election of 1860 to report for the New York Herald, *and through it for the entire membership of the Associated Press, the day-by-day doings of Abraham Lincoln. For Henry Villard was then but twenty-five and one-half years old, had been only seven years in this country, was not yet a citizen, and had not mastered the English language sufficiently to write for the vernacular press until two years before this vitally important assignment. Thus hundreds of thousands of Americans learned of the words and actions of the President-elect only through the letters of this young foreign-born reporter, who had*

v

brought to this country that ardent devotion to democracy and liberty which had made him in 1849, at fourteen years, a rebel against his king in his native Palatinate.

The telegrams and letters sent by Henry Villard which are printed in this volume have been edited hardly at all. They merit preservation not only because of the historical picture they present of Lincoln preparing for the Presidency and being overrun by the curious and the office-seekers who stormed Springfield and stole from him precious hours needed for rest, for planning, for contemplation. They deserve republication also because of the amazing mastery of the medium by one so young and so new to the language, and the vividness of the reports, and because of the testimony they bear to the effect upon Henry Villard of his daily association with one who was so soon to be of the immortals. As the dispatches show, this youthful correspondent at first expressed doubt as to whether Lincoln could rise to the gravest national emergency. Within a month Henry Villard admitted his error, recognized the worth of the man he daily portrayed and recorded his belief that the North had found the great leader the crisis called

for—*an admission most creditable to the reporter
who at twenty-five could recognize the pure gold
beneath Lincoln's rough exterior and could visualize
correctly just what qualities the saviour-to-be of
the Republic must possess.*

*Grateful acknowledgement is made here of the
permission given by the* Saturday Evening Post
*to reprint that portion of the dispatches which ap-
peared in its issue of February 10, 1940 under the
title "Lincoln At Bay." If there has been in the ar-
rangement an apparent departure from the chrono-
logical order, it is mainly due to the fact that some
of the letters were telegraphed and some were
mailed. In each case the date of their dispatching
has been used and not the date of publication in the*
Herald. *It is especially worth recording that the*
Herald, *although then published in a day of extreme journalistic partisanship and itself bitterly
and violently opposed to Lincoln and to his election, never sought to interfere with or to edit the
dispatches of its Springfield correspondent. It let
him praise Lincoln as he saw fit.*

*In order to give the proper background of Henry
Villard's friendship with Lincoln his earlier meetings with Lincoln have been collected in the Pro-*

logue from Mr. Villard's autobiography, published by Houghton Mifflin & Company in 1904. The Epilogue contains his account of Lincoln's inauguration.

HAROLD G. VILLARD

OSWALD GARRISON VILLARD

December, 1940

CONTENTS

✵

LINCOLN ON THE EVE

of '61

Henry Villard's Meetings with Lincoln Prior to November, 1860

Mr. Villard reported in German four of the Lincoln-Douglas debates for the New York *Staats-Zeitung*. He attended the first of the series at Ottawa, Illinois, on August 21, 1858, but it was not until the Freeport debate, the second, on August 27, that he was introduced to Lincoln and "found him most approachable, good natured and full of wit and humor." Lincoln on the platform Mr. Villard in later life described as follows:

As far as all external conditions were concerned, there was nothing in favor of Lincoln. He had a lean, lank, indescribably gawky figure, an odd-featured, wrinkled, inexpressive, and altogether uncomely face. He used singularly awkward, almost absurd, up-and-down and sidewise movements of his body to give emphasis to his arguments. His voice was naturally good, but he frequently raised it to an unnatural pitch. Yet the unprejudiced mind felt at once that, while there was on the one side a skilful dialectician and debater arguing a wrong and weak cause, there was on the other a thoroughly earnest and truthful man, inspired by sound convictions in consonance with the true spirit of American institutions. There was nothing at all in Douglas's powerful effort that appealed to the higher instincts of human nature, while Lincoln always touched sympathetic chords. Lincoln's speech excited and sustained the enthusiasm of his audience to the end. When he had finished, two stalwart young farmers rushed on the platform, and, in spite of his remonstrances, seized and put him on their shoulders and carried him in that uncomfortable posture for a considerable distance. It was a really ludicrous sight to see the grotesque figure holding frantically on to the heads of his supporters, with his legs dangling from their shoulders, and his pantaloons pulled up so as to expose his underwear almost to his knees. Douglas made dexterous use of this incident in his next speech, expressing sincere regret that, against his wish, he had used up his old friend Lincoln so completely that he had to be carried off the stage. Lincoln retaliated by saying at the first opportunity that he had known Judge Douglas long and well, but there was nevertheless one thing he could not say of him, and that was that the Judge always told the truth. . . .

I firmly believe that, if Stephen A. Douglas had lived, he would have had a brilliant national career. . . . As I took final leave of him and Lincoln, doubtless neither of them had any idea that within two years they would be rivals again in the Presidential race. I had it from Lincoln's own lips that the United States Senatorship was the greatest political height he at the time expected to climb. He was full of doubt, too, of his ability to secure the majority of the Legislature against Douglas. These confidences he imparted to me on a special occasion which I must not omit to mention in detail. . . .

He and I met accidentally, about nine o'clock on a hot, sultry evening, at a flag railroad station about twenty miles west of Springfield, on my re-

turn from a great meeting at Petersburg in Menard
County. He had been driven to the station in a
buggy and left there alone. I was already there.
The train that we intended to take for Springfield
was about due. After vainly waiting for half an
hour for its arrival, a thunderstorm compelled us to
take refuge in an empty freight-car standing on a
side track, there being no buildings of any sort at
the station. We squatted down on the floor of the
car and fell to talking on all sorts of subjects. It was
then and there he told me that, when he was clerk-
ing in a country store, his highest political ambition
was to be a member of the State Legislature. "Since
then, of course," he said laughingly, "I have grown
some, but my friends got me into *this* business
[*meaning the canvass*]. I did not consider myself
qualified for the United States Senate, and it took
me a long time to persuade myself that I was. Now,
to be sure," he continued, with another of his pe-
culiar laughs, "I am convinced that I am good
enough for it; but, in spite of it all, I am saying to
myself every day: 'It is too big a thing for you;
you will never get it.' Mary insists, however, that
I am going to be Senator and President of the United
States, too." These last words he followed with a

roar of laughter, with his arms around his knees, and shaking all over with mirth at his wife's ambition. "Just think," he exclaimed, "of such a sucker as me as President!"

He then fell to asking questions regarding my antecedents, and expressed some surprise at my fluent use of English after so short a residence in the United States. Next he wanted to know whether it was true that most of the educated people in Germany were "infidels." I answered that they were not openly professed infidels, but such a conclusion might be drawn from the fact that most of them were not church-goers. "I do not wonder at that," he rejoined; "my own inclination is that way." I ventured to give expression to my own disbelief in the doctrine of the Christian church relative to the existence of God, the divinity of Christ, and immortality. This led him to put other questions to me to draw me out. He did not commit himself, but I received the impression that he was of my own way of thinking. It was no surprise to me, therefore, to find in the writings of his biographers Ward Hill Lamon and W. H. Herndon that I had correctly understood him. Our talk continued till half-past ten, when the belated train arrived. I cherish this ac-

cidental rencontre as one of my most precious
recollections, since my companion of that night has
become one of the greatest figures in history.

In 1859 Henry Villard, then representing the
Cincinnati *Commercial*, was the only passenger
in the first stage-coach from Fort Leavenworth
to Denver, the new mining camp at Cherry
Creek. Later, with Horace Greeley of the *Trib-
une*, and Albert D. Richardson, of the Boston
Journal, he gave the first reliable certification of
the existence of gold in Colorado. Returning to
the East in the Fall of 1859 in a two-horse wagon
with two companions, he had the following
encounter on a November day in Missouri:

About thirty miles from St. Joseph an extraordinary incident occurred. A buggy with two occupants was coming toward us over the open prairie.
As it approached, I thought I recognized one of
them, and, sure enough, it turned out to be no less
a person than Abraham Lincoln! I stopped the
wagon, called him by name, and jumped off to
shake hands. He did not recognize me with my full
beard and pioneer's costume. When I said, "Don't

you know me?" and gave my name, he looked at me, most amazed, and then burst out laughing. "Why, good gracious! you look like a real Pike's-Peaker." His surprise at this unexpected meeting was as great as mine. He was on a lecturing tour through Kansas. It was a cold morning, and the wind blew cuttingly from the northwest. He was shivering in the open buggy, without even a roof over it, in a short overcoat, and without any covering for his legs. I offered him one of my buffalo robes, which he gratefully accepted. He undertook, of course, to return it to me, but I never saw it again. After ten minutes' chat, we separated. The next time I saw him he was the Republican candidate for the Presidency.

I

Lincoln at Springfield,

from November 16, 1860 on

Having visited Springfield often in 1858 and during the Presidential campaign, Henry Villard had many acquaintances there including Richard Yates, who had just been elected Governor, Judge Logan, Lincoln's law partner, Jesse K. Dubois, the State Auditor, and the editors of the local dailies. He wrote that on his arrival in the middle of November Lincoln "gave me a very friendly welcome, and authorized me to come to him at any time for any information I needed." Of this permission Mr. Villard often availed himself. He found during his three months of daily association with Lincoln that while the latter was always ready to talk with him on the question of secession the

President-elect refused to commit himself to any
definite policy. Henry Villard was often present
at conversations and conferences between Lincoln and leading public men in which this question of the dismemberment of the Republic came
up, and found that with them, too, Lincoln confined himself to generalizations, but never hesi-
tated to say that the Union ought to be and in
his opinion would be preserved, though at
times he had his doubts whether this could be
done even by force. "No one," Mr. Villard wrote
in his memoirs, "who heard him talk upon the
other question [secession] could fail to discover
his 'other side' and to be impressed with his deep
earnestness, his anxious contemplation of public affairs, and his thorough sense of the extraordinary responsibilities that were coming upon
him."

According to Mr. Villard, "Springfield was
then a small but attractive town of some nine
thousand inhabitants. The business part cen-
tered in the square in which stood the State
House, with the offices of the Governor and the
heads of departments and the legislative cham-

bers. The residence streets extended at right an-
gles from the square. None of the streets were
paved, and in wet weather, of which a good
deal prevailed during that winter, they were
simply impassable. There was but one decent
hotel, where I put up, and this became the
principal stopping place of thousands of visitors, who, from curiosity or for political consultation and place-hunting, made a pilgrimage to
this transient Mecca during the succeeding
months." Mr. Lincoln had found soon after his
election that his simple two-storey wooden
house was altogether inadequate for the throngs
who came to see him, and so he gladly availed
himself of the Governor's offer to let him use the
Governor's room in the Capitol. When Mr. Villard arrived he found that Lincoln was already
spending a good part of each day in it.

In his first letter of November 16, 1860, Mr.
Villard declared that while "a new sun has risen
on the political horizon" the "political satellites"
eager for the division of the spoils had not yet
appeared, only hordes of the curious who came
merely to gaze and gape. But two days later the

place-seekers were there. The next day he
wrote of the former:

    Small as the number of attendants has been
for some days—not over 160 per day—the receptions of the President are nevertheless highly interesting and worthy of detailed notice. They are held
daily from ten A.M. to 12 Noon and from three
P.M. to half-past five P.M. in the Governor's room at
the State House, which has been for some time
given up to the wants of Mr. Lincoln.

    The appointed hour having arrived, the crowd
moved up stairs into the second storey, in the south-
east corner of which the reception room is located.
Passing through a rather dark sort of doorway, the
clear voice and often ringing laughter of the President usually guide them to the right door. The bold-
est of the party having knocked, a ready "Come in"
invites them to enter. On opening the door, the tall,
lean form of "Old Abe" directly confronts the leader
of the party. Seizing the latter's hand with a hearty
shake, Lincoln leads him in, and bids the rest to
follow suit with an encouraging "Get in, all of you."
The whole party being in, he will ask for their
names, and then immediately start a running con-

versation. Although he is naturally more listened
to than talked to, he does not allow a pause to become protracted. He is never at a loss as to the
subjects that please the different classes of visitors
and there is a certain quaintness and originality
about all he has to say, so that one cannot help
feeling interested. His "talk" is not brilliant. His
phrases are not ceremoniously set, but pervaded
with a humorousness and, at times, with a grotesque
joviality, that will always please. I think it would
be hard to find one who tells better jokes, enjoys
them better and laughs oftener than Abraham
Lincoln.

The room of the Governor of the State of
Illinois cannot be said to indicate the vast terri-
torial extent of that commonwealth. It is altogether
inadequate for the accommodation of Mr. Lincoln's
visitors. Twenty persons will not find standing
room in it, and the simultaneous presence of a
dozen only will cause inconvenience. The room is
furnished with a sofa, half-a-dozen armchairs, a
table and a desk, the latter being assigned to the
private secretary, who is always present during visiting hours. These, together with countless letters
and files of newspapers, and quite an assortment of

odd presents, constitute the only adornments of the apartment. No restrictions, whatever, being exercised as to visitors, the crowd, that daily waits on the President, is always of a motley description. Everybody who lives in this vicinity or passes through this place, goes to take a look at "Old Abe." Muddy boots and hickory shirts are just as frequent as broadcloth, fine linen, etc. The ladies, however, are usually dressed up in their very best, although they cannot hope to make an impression on old married Lincoln. Offensively democratic exhibitions of free manners occur every once in a while. Churlish fellows will obtrude themselves with their hats on, lighted cigars and their pantaloons tucked into their boots. Dropping into chairs they sit puffing away and trying to gorgonize the President with their silent stares, until their boorish curiosity is fully satisfied. Formal presentations are dispensed with in most cases. Nearly everyone finds his own way in and introduces himself. Sometimes half a dozen rustics rush in, break their way through other visitors up to the object of their search and after calling their names and touching the Presidential fingers, back out again.

November 19

His old friends, who have been used to a great indifference as to the "outer man" on his part, say that "Abe is putting on airs." By this, they refer to the fact that he is now wearing a brand new hat and suit and that he has commenced cultivating the—with him—unusual adornment of whiskers.

But, these late outward embellishments to the contrary notwithstanding, a Broadway tailor would probably feel no more tempted to consider Lincoln as coming up to his artistic requirements of a model man than Peter Cooper. The angularity of the Presidential form, and its habitual *laissez aller*, preclude a like possibility. We venture to say that Fifth Avenue snobs, if unaware who he was, would be horrified at walking across the street with him. And yet, there is something about the man that makes one at once forget these exterior short-comings and feel attracted toward him.

The President-elect being the very embodiment of good humor, it seems as though from this fact, much that happens about him partakes of a comical character. Some days ago, a tall Missourian marched into the reception room. Seeing the tall form of the President rise before him, and not knowing what to say, he ejaculated "I reckon one is about as big as the other." "Let us measure" was the instantaneous reply; and the Missourian was actually placed against the wall, told "to be honest, and stand flat on his heels," and his height measured with a stick.

Mr. Lincoln's personal appearance is the subject of daily remark among those who have known him formerly. Always cadaverous, his aspect is now almost ghostly. His position is wearing him terribly. Letters threatening his life are daily received from the South, occasionally, also, a note of warning from some Southerner who does not like his principles, but would regret violence. But these trouble him little compared with the apprehended difficulty of conciliating the South without destroying the integrity of his own party. The present aspect of the country, I think, augurs one of the most difficult terms which any President has yet been called to weather; and I doubt Mr. Lincoln's capacity for the task of bringing light and peace out of the chaos that will surround him. A man of good heart and good intention, he is not firm. The times demand a Jackson.

November 20

Today's work was the hardest "Old Abe" did
since his election. He had hardly appeared at the
State House when he was beset by an eager crowd
that had been on the lookout for him ever since
daylight. They gave him no time to occupy himself the usual two hours previous to the morning
receptions with his private secretary, but clung to
his coat tails with an obstinacy worthy of a better cause. He had to admit them at once into his
apartment, and then submit for nearly ten long,
weary hours to the importunities of a steady tide of
callers. Limited as the space required by the lean
proportions of the President is, he found it a most
difficult task to find sufficient standing room. By
constant entreaties to make room he maintained
himself in close proximity to the door, which position he had chosen with a view to facilitating the
inevitable hand shakings. But he found to his intense bodily inconvenience that this deference to
the comfort of his callers was not the most practi-
cal plan he might have adopted. The curious de-
filed past him, after squeezing the Presidential
fingers, into the room, and settled either on the

sofa or chairs or remained standing for protracted observations. Only after having stared with open mouths to their heart's content—many employed hours in that agreeable pastime—would they move out of the room and enable others to gain admittance. A tight jam prevailed, therefore, all day around the President, who found himself frequently "driven to the wall."

Many Sangamon country youths brought their sweethearts along and presented them to "Old Abe," who was at times surrounded by robust beauty. Place seekers were in despair all day. In vain, they tried to gain the Presidential ear. It was monopolized from early morning until late in the evening by the "people."

Although "Old Abe" had been nearly tortured to death during the daytime, the people gave him no rest after dark; even at his private residence, at half-past six, he was once more crowded upon in his parlor, and had to undergo another agony of presentations. The whole lower story of the building was filled all the evening with well dressed ladies and gentlemen, whose comfort was, however, greatly diminished by the constant influx of an ill-mannered populace. Mrs. Lincoln had to en-

dure as many importunities as the head of the
family. She often had to hear callers ask each
other, "Is that the old woman?" The President's off-
spring, however, seemed to enjoy the fuss hugely.
The cheering outside was always responded to by
their juvenile yells.

As predicted by me some days ago, the Republican jollification of today was, as to display of
enthusiasm and number of attendance, a comparative failure, although held at the capital of the State
and the home of the President-elect. The American
people are known not to be able to foster a protracted excitement on one particular subject. Having been treated *ad nauseam* to wide awake pro-
cessions, meetings, speeches, fireworks, etc., during
the campaign, they are now sick of all such empty
demonstrations, and wish to see no more of them
for some time. The aggregate number of attendants
from abroad did not exceed two thousand, and that
of actual participants fell below five hundred.

Chicago, November 21

Mr. Lincoln, the President-elect, left Springfield for this city at 11 o'clock this forenoon, accompanied by Mrs. Lincoln, Senator Trumbull and

family, and Don Piatt and wife, of Ohio. Mr. Lincoln purchased his tickets and travelled in a crowded and inconvenient car like other democratic sovereigns, neither the company nor conductor showing him any courtesy whatever, although the same corporation recently treated a foreign prince [*the Prince of Wales, later Edward the VII*] to a special train over their road. The conductor permitted ironed convicts, one a murderer, to enter the car and take seats between the families of Mr. Lincoln and of Senator Trumbull. The sheriff having the culprits in charge is a Douglas Democrat.

Springfield, November 26

Mr. Lincoln returned this evening from Chicago with his family. He looks rather the worse for wear but has preserved the even tenor of his temper, the incessant importunities of place seekers in the North to the contrary notwithstanding. If he expects relief here he will be disappointed. A number of expectants have been lying in wait for him during the last twenty-four hours, who will swoop upon him in the morning with an eagerness doubled by the delay.

Lincoln's trip to Chicago in the company of Senator Trumbull is of especial significance because of a remarkable address made by the Senator in Springfield on November 20, the day before he journeyed with Lincoln to Chicago. The President-elect had stated that he would not take any position at that time on the grave question of secession which at that moment was actually disrupting the Union. The pressure of events and men upon him became so great, however, that he changed his mind. But instead of speaking out himself he authorized Senator Trumbull to speak for him. The Senator declared that secession was impracticable, or rather an impossibility. Said he: "The Constitution provides no way by which a State may withdraw from the Union—no way for the dissolution of the government." He also stated, however, that the Federal Government has "no more right to meddle with slavery in a State than it has to interfere with serfdom in Russia." Two days later Henry Villard explained the President's change of mind in the following dispatch, undoubtedly written after consultation with

Lincoln. It is of special importance because it showed the pressure being brought to bear on Lincoln during these Springfield days when he permitted his time and strength to be wasted to so great a degree by the curious and the office seekers although events were in the making which threatened the life of the Republic. The dispatch of November 22 reads:

Stubborn facts of the most fearful portent were daily developed since the eventful sixth day of the month. They stared at the newly made President with all their ill-boding earnestness. He could not possibly shut his eyes to their growing gravity. He could not block his mind to their serious logic. Every newspaper he opened was filled with clear indications of an impending national catastrophe. Every mail brought him written, and every hour verbal, entreaties to abandon his paralyzed silence, repress untimely feelings of delicacy, and pour the oil of conciliatory conservative assurances upon the turbulent waves of Southern excitement. Even among his own political adherents, many Union loving men exhorted him to yield. But a few steps from his reception room, the leading financiers of the State were assembled for many days to counsel and devise the best means of averting the commercial crisis threatened by the unexampled decline of the various State stocks, on which the paper currency—the vital foundation of Western commerce—was based. Telegraphic dispatches, conveying the troubles and anxieties of Eastern financial commercial centers, constantly flashed upon him. Would it have been possible for any man in whose breast even but a solitary spark of patriotism glimmered, to remain unmoved and withhold the relief asked of him, when appealed to so continuously and urgently? Whatever the political inclinations of the President-elect may be, he is fortunately possessed of a large heart and hence could not, at the sight of the wrong and misery [*existing*] and about being engendered, fail to respond in the desired manner.

While Mr. Lincoln was away the reporter recalled the extraordinary change in his fortunes:

November 26

Just about two years ago, the writer was accidentally obliged to stop a day in this city. Partly from curiosity and partly from a natural sympathy with misfortune he felt induced to pay a visit to Old Abe Lincoln. He found him sitting solitary and alone in his dingy, dusty law office. He had been baffled but a short time before in his powerful and protracted struggle with the "Little Giant" for the latter's seat in the United States Senate. The only spoils he had carried off in that momentous contest were a pile of campaign documents, rising to his right. But loss of time and labor, disappointed hopes and thwarted aspirations did not seem to grate upon his mind. He was resigned. He knew that he had made a good fight—no matter what the result. His talk was cheerful. His wit and humor had not deserted him. Altogether, he was a striking variation from the picture usually presented by unsuccessful aspirants to office.

At the same time a different scene was enacted not over a hundred yards from his office. In a spacious room in the second storey of a three storey brick building on the east side of the public square, a hilarious, exulting company was assembled. They were the sachems of the Illinois democracy, who had assembled in their time honored Wigwam— the Tammany Hall of the Prairie State—to rejoice

over the triumph of their chieftain [*Douglas*]. The
flash of victory gleamed from their eyes. Party zeal,
intensified by free indulgence in things spirituous,
animated their countenances. Eloquent words of
congratulation flowed from their lips, and well
enough it was for them to be jubilant. The political world looked their own. An unobstructed path
to the Presidency appeared to be open to their
leader. He seemed the man of the day. His prospect of being elevated to the highest office in the
land was evidently certain. No wonder, then, that
they were brim-full of hopeful expectations and
elated at the coming "good times."

But times change and so do men and matters.
The other day I repeated my visit to the same
locality. Alas! as with your Tammany its glory has
departed. The jubilant crowd of yore was wanting.
A table, a few armchairs, a collection of empty
bottles and a bust of the vanquished champion of
popular sovereignty—not veiled in mourning but in
thick layers of dust—were now the only occupants
of the hallowed spot. And all this at a time when he,
whose defeat once caused it to resound with lusty
cheers, was receiving directly opposite the hom-

age of those that have placed him at the head of the nation, and disowned the victor of '58.

Mr. Lincoln returned immediately to his former way of life after his brief outing:

November 28

Immediately after his arrival from Chicago on Monday evening last, the President-elect repaired to his reception room to open and digest his accumulated correspondence. A pile of letters greeted him before which a less determined soul might well have quailed. Until late last night and all day yesterday did it absorb all his attention. With a creditable patience he waded through the contents of several hundred letters, the perusal of which made him no wiser. Even his keen sense of the ludicrous begins to be blunted by the frequency of its imitation. Bad grammar and worse penmanship, stylistic originality, frankness of thought and pertinence of expression, vain glorious assurance and impudent attempts at exaction may do well enough for the temporary excitement of humor. Mr. Lincoln's correspondence would offer a most abundant source of

knowledge to the student of human nature. It
emanates from representatives of all grades of
society. The grave effusions of statesmen; the disinterested advice of patriots reach him simultaneously with the well-calculated, wheedling praises
of the expectant politician and the meaningless
commonplaces of scribblers from mere curiosity.
Female forwardness and inquisitiveness are frequently brought to his notice. Exuberant "wide
awake" enthusiasm, with difficulty pressed into the
narrow forms of a letter, is lavished upon him.
Poets hasten to tax their muse in his glorification.
A perfect shower of "able editorials" is clipped out
and enclosed. Artists express their happiness in
supplying him with wretched wood-cut representa-
tions of his surroundings. Authors and speculative
book-sellers freely send their congratulations, accompanied by complimentary volumes. Inventors
are exceedingly liberal with circulars and samples.
More impulsive than well-mannered, Southerners
indulge in occasional missives containing senseless
fulminations and, in a few instances, disgraceful
threats and indecent drawings. A goodly number of
seditious pamphlets and manifestoes has also arrived—in fine all the "light and shadow" of Anglo-

American political humanity is reflected by the hundreds of letters daily received by the President-elect.

But few visitors diverted Mr. Lincoln from his correspondence yesterday. Some old acquaintances, of twenty and more years' standing, called on him in the morning, and engaged in a lively discussion of the past and the present. He led them back to the period of his first public services in the Legislature of this State, in the years of 1837 and 1838 and dwelt with evident satisfaction on the time when he and eight other sixfooters—universally known in those days as the "long nine" —represented this section in that body. He told the story of the Kentucky Justice of the Peace whose first case was a criminal prosecution for the abuse of slaves. Unable to find any precedents he exclaimed at last angrily: "I will be damned if I don't feel almost sorry for being elected when the niggers is the first thing I have to attend to." This story was Lincoln's reply to a visitor's regret that the vexatious slavery matter would have to be the first matter of public policy for Lincoln to deal with in Washington.

In the course of the day "Old Abe" was in-

duced to give an account of the sights he had seen
in Chicago. He did it with his usual grotesque *bon
hommie*. His sketch of the dinner and other parties,
and the Sunday school meetings he had to attend—
of the crowds of the curious that importuned him at
all hours of the day, of the public levees he was
obliged to hold, etc., was graphic. It seems that
instead of enjoying rest and relief, as expected, he
was even more molested than in this place. If
people only knew his holy horror of public ovations,
they would probably treat him more sparingly. To
be lugged around from place to place to satisfy the
curiosity of the populace, is a doubtful mode of be-
stowing honor and rendering homage, etc. Mr.
Lincoln's experience at Chicago will probably deter
him from undertaking another journey previous to
his final departure for Washington City. [*It did.*]

November 29

A lot of country people came in on Thanksgiv-
ing Day. One garrulous old lady said she well re-
membered Abe when still a boy in his old home in
Kentucky. She expressed great astonishment at his
elevation to the highest office in the land. "Why,"
she said, "he was the gawkiest, dullest looking boy

you ever saw," but she added: "There was one thing remarkable about him. He could always remember things better than any other boy in the neighborhood."

The best evidence of Mr. Lincoln's popularity in this vicinity where he has lived for nearly thirty years, is furnished by the fact that it is almost impossible to converse with any old resident about him without eliciting one or more stories illustrative of his ever ready wit, inexhaustible humor, quick repartee, honest frankness and good understanding with everybody. One could with ease collect a volume of personal anecdotes by a week's canvass of the lawyers' offices, court rooms, State and county offices, etc., in search of similar information. Only last night a democrat of twenty years' standing treated me to an incident of this kind. Some twenty-three years ago when Lincoln was doing this State his first service, in the capacity of a member of the lower branch of the General Assembly, the legislators saw fit to raise their per diem from two to four dollars. The passage of this measure excited a good deal of feeling in those poor times. It was thought entirely uncalled for, extravagant and an outrage upon the taxpayers of the State.

Lincoln had to endure a good deal of denunciation upon that score upon his return. One day an old acquaintance, in the shape of a blunt, hard working yeoman, met him and also commenced remonstrating about the same matter. He could and would not understand why men should be paid four dollars per day for "doing nothing but talking and sitting on benches," while he averaged only about one for the hardest kind of work. Having fully given vent to his feelings, he wound up at last with an angry, "Now, Abe, I want to know what in the world made you do it?" Nothing daunted by the dissatisfaction of his constituent, "Abe" replied instanter, "I reckon the only reason was that we wanted the money."

II

Lincoln Faces Disunion
—and Grows

December 5

The symposium of the President's message sent to the press was read by Mr. Lincoln this morning. He very freely gave vent to his surprise at its tenor, as it plainly revealed, in his opinion, Mr. Buchanan's desire to rest the whole responsibility of the secession movement on the Free States. He expressed himself likewise in strong language on that part that refers to himself, as he says it entirely misrepresents his views. [*Later a fuller report of the Message modified Mr. Lincoln's indignation somewhat.*]

December 11

While the confusion, commotion and danger is greater from day to day in the political arena,

the President-elect maintains his equanimity undis-
turbed. Quietly, fulfilling what he considers his
present duties, he faces events with a philosophic
calmness. Not that he does not feel intense anxiety
as to what the future has in store for the people of
this country; on the contrary, not a move on the
public stage escapes his attention nor fails to be
clearly appreciated. But he evidently entertains
the conviction that he can do nothing that is likely
to stem the tide of the times. What is asked of him
in the way of public definitions of his policy, he
would probably give if he could persuade himself
that it would do aught toward the adjustment of
the present troubles. But he considers all such
demonstrations futile, as the South, to use his own
language, "has eyes but does not see, and ears but
does not hear." As to the announcement of the composition of his Cabinet, it has been rendered impossible by the attitude of the South. How can he
select three, or whatever number of its members
may be determined upon from that section, when
the same men may be made foreigners by the progress of disunion even before the inauguration of his
Administration? How can he for this reason, on

the other hand, choose but Northern men without adding fuel to the secession flame?

December 7

However prejudiced by partisan bias the daily observer of Mr. Lincoln's doings might be, he could not resist the impression that all he does and thinks bears the stamp of conscientiousness and solicitous dutifulness. It would be sheer falsification, indeed, to deny that he entertains a sincere anxiety, not so much as to the special interests of the party that elected him, and the furtherance of his own fortunes, as with regard to his duties to the country at large and the means of discharging them to the best of his power and ability. I venture to say that none has passed out of his reception room without being firmly convinced that he honestly means to sink the man in the public officer, the partisan in the patriot, the Republican in the faithful protector of the federal laws in every State of the republic.

This being the case, it only remains to be seen whether circumstances will not prove too strong for him—whether he will simply float on the current of events or prove able to direct their course, as far as his official power goes. Giving him credit for honesty of purpose, we only know Mr. Lincoln in addition to being a strong debater, [*to be*] a good dialectician, a well informed politician and a sound lawyer. What his executive abilities are we still have to learn. These are great and perilous times, and great must be the man for them. The stuff of which he is made must be as stern as the aspect of our days. Mediocrity will no longer do. The innermost resources of the highest statesmanship will be required. Illusion will be no more in place. Difficulties will have to be looked boldly and squarely in the face. To believe, then, as I do, that Mr. Lincoln will be found but little wanting in these several respects, is certainly no mean source of gratification. Having closely observed him since the election, and well noted the impressions made upon him by the secession phases of the present imbroglio, I dare say that there are dormant qualities in "Old Abe" which occasion will draw forth, develop and remind people to a certain degree of the characteristics of "Old Hickory." . . .

Whether the sequence will bear out my judgment or not, an earnest of his high sense of the requirements of his position at least will be found in the fact that he is indefatigable in his efforts to arrive at the fullest comprehension of the present situation of public affairs and the most proper conclusions as to its probable consequences. He never contents himself with a superficial opinion based on newspaper accounts and arguments, but always fortifies his position by faithful researches for precedents, analogies, authorities, etc. He is at all times surrounded by piles of standard works to which constant reference is made. His strong desire for full and reliable information on all current topics renders it especially regretful to him that circumstances debar him from obtaining anything but ex parte statements as to the progress of events in the South.

As the 4th of March is drawing near, the impending removal to the federal capital becomes more and more the subject of discussion and preparation with the President-elect and his family. It is true his worldly goods are so few that their disposition will hardly cause him any great embarrassment. It is, however, but natural that the prospective exodus from the town with which his life has been identified for over a quarter of a century should produce some mental tribulation. Mr.

Lincoln himself has as yet devoted only thoughts to this matter; but the lady members of his family are said to be already busily engaged in preparing for a becoming entrance into the White House. That present haunt of a lonely bachelor promises to be greatly enlivened after the inauguration of the new administration. Mrs. Lincoln's youthfulness will bring about a revolution.

December 14

The appearance of Mr. Lincoln has somewhat changed to the worse within the last week. He does not complain of any direct ailment, but that he looks more pale and careworn than heretofore is evident to the daily observer. But, whatever effect his new responsibilities may have had upon his body, the vigor of his mind and the steadiness of his humorous disposition are obviously unimpaired.

December 16

If I were asked upon what element in the composition of the President-elect I looked upon as the most likely source of apprehension, I would not mention in reply either his wrongly imputed hostility towards the South, nor the alleged aggressiveness of the party that elected him and expects faithfulness on his part to its tenets. Nay, off as it may sound, I would name on the contrary a quality which is by common consent considered rather laudable than otherwise—viz.: his good nature.

To receive everybody with uniform kindness —to indulge the general curiosity with untiring patience—to reply to all questions with unvarying readiness—to grant willing compliance to all requests—to hold endless suggestions—may be a very good and pleasing rule in private life. It is doubtlessly, likewise, an effective means of popularity in public spheres; but its general observation by so high-stationed a personage as the President of the United States, I venture to say, is fraught with many hazards and that from the very abuse of those for whose benefit it is practiced.

All that can claim the personal acquaintance of Mr. Lincoln will agree that he is the very embodiment of good temper and affability. They will all concede that he has a kind word, an encouraging smile, a humorous remark for nearly everyone that seeks his presence, and that but few, if any, emerge from his reception room without being strongly and favorably impressed with his general disposition. But, although his visitors may leave him all thus well pleased is it not more than probable that the pleasure is only one sided and unshared by him that produced it? It is true that no man enjoys company more than Mr. Lincoln. It is true he loves argument, discussion, witty sayings, etc., perhaps as much as any mortal. But it may be, nevertheless, safely presumed that the sensations derived from his variegated intercourse are not all of an agreeable character, but that, on the contrary, they were largely intermingled with annoyance and perplexity.

Yet notwithstanding the assertions of sensation writers—that never failing plague of political eminence in this country—the grovelling time-wasters, fawners, sycophants and parasites combined in the genus "office seekers" have thus far affected him only in a slight degree. From present appearances, indeed, it may be inferred that it will not be visited upon him in all its virulence until after his advent in the White House. Delay and the unwelcome distance having sharpened their appetites, the place-wanting cormorants will then beset him in close file and with double fury. Reticence will then have to supersede, to some extent, unrestrained communicativeness. Reserve must take the place of indiscriminating affability. His ears and eyes must learn to be closed at certain times. His lips must be trained to less ready and unqualified responses. If not, the crowd will unbalance and overwhelm him.

December 19

Considerable sensation was produced today in the Capitol by the appearance of a live disunionist, wearing the emblem of secession. The gentleman who calls himself D. E. Ray, and claimed to be from Yazoo, Miss., stalked into Mr. Lincoln's reception room with a blue cockade displayed upon his hat. He walked in with a sullen air, introduced himself and plunged into a corner of the sofa, where he reposed for at least a quarter of an hour, without uttering a word, and with his eyes down, but all the while manipulating his tile so as to fasten the President's eye upon the cockade. Mr. Lincoln at first hardly noticed him; but one of the other visitors addressed some questions to the scowling Southron that induced him to open his lips. The conversation soon turned to the secession issue. In its course the Mississippian remarked gruffly that they were not afraid down South of Mr. Lincoln himself, but of those who followed him.

The President-elect hereupon joined in the talk, and soon found occasion to remark that "the main differences between Northerners and Southerners were that the former held slavery to be wrong and opposed its further extension, while the latter thought it right and endeavored to spread it; that, although the republicans were anti-extensionists, they would not interfere with slavery where it existed, and that as to his own intentions, the slave States would find that their slave property would be as secure from encroachments as it had been under Mr. Buchanan." The Southron, having evidently softened down under the influence of these peaceful declarations, requested of Mr. Lincoln a copy of the debates with Senator Douglas, which was duly given him, with an inscription by the donor upon the title page. Mr. Lincoln remarked, on handing the book to him, that he hoped its possession would not give him any trouble on his return to Mississippi.

December 24

About two weeks ago I took occasion to state in a letter to the *Herald* that invitations had been sent out from here to divers political eminences to repair hither for the purpose of both consulting with the President-elect on the present condition of public affairs and receiving offers of seats in the Cabinet. This announcement is now being rapidly verified. A week since Mr. Edward Bates made his appearance and was tendered the Secretaryship of the Interior. Last Thursday Thurlow Weed loomed up, to return with the authority to sound certain New York gentlemen as to their willingness to serve, and today David Wilmot, of Proviso renown, made his advent, to become the recipient of the flattering offer of a place among Mr. Lincoln's constitutional advisers.

Simultaneously with Mr. Wilmot, Col. E. D. Baker, the newly elected Senator from Oregon, arrived in this his old home, his first visit since his emigration to the Pacific coast some ten years ago. "Ned," as he was familiarly called hereabouts in

former days, was most cordially greeted, by his old
friend, the President-elect, and a host of relatives
and acquaintances. His visit is of a purely private
character. . . .

December 25

Mr. Wilmot having left, Senator Baker is the
sole observed of all Springfield observers. He is
certainly a remarkable man and has made a remarkable career. Of restless ambition, indomitable
energy, true English perseverance, fine natural
parts, great elegance and popular manners, he
could not well fail to make his mark. Nor will he
go anywhere without attracting general attention.
[*Col. Edward D. Baker fell in the Battle of Ball's
Bluff, October 21, 1861, when commanding the
First California Infantry.*]

December 25

This being Christmas day . . . a good many
country people are in town but few find their way
to Mr. Lincoln's reception room. This afternoon
a party of St. Louis gentlemen all but monopolized
the attention of the President-elect.

The noon train from the East landed among us no less a personage than the greatest of Pennsylvania wirepullers, the renowned General Simon Cameron. The unexpected arrival of the General was somewhat of a stunner, not only to your correspondent but to a majority of the political schemers and intriguants in Springfield. "Proviso Dave" had been here but a few days ago. He was supposed—nay, seriously believed on the very best authority—to have been offered a place among Mr. Lincoln's constitutional advisers. The universal impression was that he had promptly and gladly accepted the flattering tender. What, then, did Cameron's sudden apparition mean? Was the Keystone State to be rewarded for the republican laurels it had won so gloriously by a double representation in the Cabinet? An altogether improbable inference. . . . But although your correspondent is as yet without positive information on the subject he ventures to express the unshaken conviction that Mr. Cameron will not occupy a seat in the Cabinet. He may be mistaken in this. But, if so, the error will be excusable as it is based on the well known rigid adherence to honesty of both purpose and means of the President-elect, and the presumption that he, as a well informed politician, cannot be ignorant of the character of the agents employed by Cameron in promoting his political fortunes.

January 1

The fog in which the object of Senator Cameron's visit was wrapped has cleared away to a certain extent since my last. It is now certain that his journey hither was prompted by the consideration of his claims to a position in the Cabinet. But although it is positively known that he came here for the purpose of settling his account with the President-elect the precise manner in which this was done has not yet transpired.

January 7

I am able to state on positive authority that Mr. Cameron has not been tendered the appointment of the Secretary of the Treasury. He came here on his own invitation, not at Mr. Lincoln's invitation, and went away disappointed. The report of his appointment was the result of intimations dropped by him here and elsewhere, and for a while was generally believed here, and by Mr. Lincoln's friends. No small indignation is felt in certain quarters that he has permitted the report to go uncontradicted and the letters which came here from Washington describing his self-satisfaction when congratulated on his elevation do not allay the irritation. [*Mr. Cameron became Secretary of War on March 4 and not head of the Treasury.*]

January 12

Although the President has been enjoying much more rest and peace since the abandonment of his daily levees than when they were in full blast, his appearance plainly indicates that an *otium cum dignitate* is not exactly the thing he is now enjoying. The concerned expression of his pallid features tells a meaningful tale. I understand that petitions and recommendations for office come upon him in daily increasing showers as the time of his inauguration approaches. The few visitors he now receives seek him in his private dwelling. To his correspondence he attends, however, with his secretary, in an office rented by him in the business part of the city.

January 16

If it be true that mirthfulness is a sign of good health, the most gratifying conclusions as to the bodily status of the President-elect may be drawn from the effect the racy leader in last Saturday's *Herald* on Cameron's discomfiture is said to have had upon the President-elect. I am informed that he laughed over it until the tears coursed down his cheeks. Bothered and perplexed as he is, the frequent application of such healthy medicine cannot but prove a relief and relaxation to him.

January 19

Few mortal beings ever carried a heavier load than that already and likely to rest hereafter, upon the shoulders of Abraham Lincoln. Nor can it be concealed that, although he stands up manfully under its weight, the burden is taxing at times his patience and power of endurance to the utmost. It is evident that he is not yet fully accustomed to the idea of being placed at the head of a nation of thirty millions of people in less than sixty days, and that the grandeur of the mission he will be called upon to fulfill is at present more than a source of anxiety and embarrassment than of hopeful and exacting emotions to him. He feels, in a measure, like one who, after groping in comparative dark, suddenly emerges upon scenes of intense brightness, and finds himself at first less at home amidst light than dimness, but gradually loses his bewilderment and realizes his position and surroundings.

It was but yesterday that I had occasion to converse with Mr. Lincoln on the subject of his impending trip to Washington City. He stated that he had as yet neither fixed the day of his departure nor selected the route, but that the former would probably take place on or about the 15th proximo. As to the latter, I think Mr. Lincoln's preferences are for a southerly route, via Cincinnati, Wheeling and Baltimore, doubtless to demonstrate how little fear he entertains for his personal safety. But there is a great pressure brought to bear on him in favor of a more northerly one, via Pittsburgh and Harrisburg, and it is most likely that this will be ultimately determined upon. Stoppages will be made by him at all the principal points. He knows that those who elected him are anxious to see how he looks, and hence is willing to gratify this, their excusable curiosity.

Since the departure of his spouse for the East, the President-elect has been keeping house alone. Whatever his other qualifications may be, it is well known that in the management of the kitchen and in other domestic concerns he is sadly destitute of both talent and experience. Hence it is more than probable that upon the return of the master spirit of his home, whose functions he so imperfectly exercises, anything but praise will be bestowed upon him for the result of his administrations during her absence.

As during the last four weeks the occupations of the President-elect consist now principally in receiving visitors, conducting negotiations for the completion of his Cabinet and attending to his correspondence. As to visitors, those that come here on his special invitation are called upon by him at their respective hotels, while those that come of their own accord are either received at his private dwelling or in his down-town office—according to their several political stations and the object of their calls. The general crowd of place seekers has to content itself with one hour each day, during which alone the Presidential ear is open to their selfish, annoying whisperings. The fact that they are hardly ever granted a separate and private hearing, but admitted into his office in a bulk, usually prevents them from making their desires and expectations known.

As to his correspondence, it has increased so wonderfully during the last fortnight that he finds it utterly impossible to read, not to speak of answering it all. I met his servant only last evening in the vestibule of the Post Office carrying a good-sized market basket full of letters. His private secretary opens them, and from the signatures determines their relative importance. Those coming from obscure sources are invariably consigned to the stove without the least mercy. Petitions for office especially share this fate.

Springfield, January 20

How many ambitious souls do not at this moment look upon Abraham Lincoln with eyes of envy? How many aspiring minds are not disposed to chide fate for placing, with comparatively little effort on his part, that highest boon immortality, within his reach, for which they vainly yearned and struggled for a lifetime? True a striking partiality has been shown to him by a power that shapes the destinies of man. The gates of fame are thrown open to him at its bidding. With a single step he is transferred from the narrow, obscure sphere of a provincial politician to the proudest position any mortal being can occupy. But there are no roses without thorns. The very luster that suddenly surrounds him may dazzle and lead him to failure and degradation. The very tide of fortune that carried him so unexpectedly to the highest place in public life may sink the inexpert steersman. Shoals and rocks without number are ahead of him, and the chances for utter wreck are equal to those for safe landing. Instead of saving the Union he may be called upon to bury it. Time, indeed, alone will decide whether the bestowal of the highest political prize within the gift of the people is justly a source of envy. . . .

I have just learned that about two weeks ago a scandalous painting on canvas was received by Mrs. Lincoln, expressed from South Carolina. It represented Mr. Lincoln with a rope around his

neck, his feet chained and his body adorned with
tar and feathers.

A number of lady friends of Mrs. Lincoln have,
with characteristic solicitude, taken up the newspaper rumors of intended attacks upon the President-elect while on his way to the Federal capital,
and used them as arguments to induce her to delay
her removal to Washington until her husband was
safely installed in the White House. But the plucky
wife of the President met all these well meant propositions with scorn, and made the spirited declara-
tion before she started on her Eastern trip that she
would see Mr. Lincoln on to Washington, danger
or no danger.

January 26

A good deal of newspaper talk has lately been
made in reference to the alleged military escort
under which Mr. Lincoln is reported to intend to
go to Washington. A company of so-called Zouaves,
lately formed in this place, is mentioned in con-
nection with this supposed martial cortège. Now,
I wish to state, for the benefit of all concerned, that
this whole story, out of which so many rude and

unjustifiable attacks upon Mr. Lincoln have
grown, has no other foundation in fact than the
conjectures, hopes and wishes of the youthful
members of the said company. The matter may
have been talked over in their drill room, and crept
into a local paper in the shape of a rumor. But
Mr. Lincoln has too much common sense to enter-
tain so ridiculous a scheme for a moment. He utterly dislikes ostentatious display and empty pageantry, and the military association referred to will
never be seen in the Federal capital if their visit is
made to depend on the pleasure of Mr. Lincoln
and the advice of all sensible friends. The raw
disciples of Mars that constitute it would certainly
afford but little real protection if such should be
wanted.

The President-elect was delighted last evening
by the arrival on the Eastern train of Mrs. Lincoln
and his oldest son, the Harvard student. He had
been awaiting their return for the last three days.
Dutiful husband and father that he is, he had pro-
ceeded to the railroad depot for three successive
nights in his anxiety to receive them, and that in
spite of snow and cold. Mrs. Lincoln returned in
good health and excellent spirits; whether she got

a good scolding from Abraham for unexpectedly prolonging her absence, I am unable to say; but I know she found it rather difficult to part with the winter gayeties of New York.

"Bob," the heir apparent to the President-elect, has been observed of all the observing Springfield girls today. He walked the streets this morning, bringing up the rear of the "old man." The effect of a residence within the improving influences of genteel, well dressed and well behaved Boston is plainly noticeable in his outward appearance, the comparative elegance of which presents a striking contrast to the loose, careless, awkward rigging of his Presidential father.

January 29

Mr. Lincoln intends to start tomorrow morning upon a two days' excursion to Charleston, the county seat of Coles county, in the southern part of this State. He proposes to pay a short visit to his aged stepmother, who resides at the point mentioned and who expressed a strong wish to see him before he left Springfield for Washington. The strictest privacy being desired by Mr. Lincoln, no reportorial shadow will follow him.

February 1

Mr. Lincoln returned home this evening after visiting his stepmother and the grave of his father at Charleston.

January 29

The pressure of place seekers from both at home and abroad continues unabated, although the President-elect is now much less disposed to allow the absorption of his now so valuable time by their selfish, provoking importunities. But neither his coolness nor his anger nor the various devices he has resorted to within the last fortnight to keep the expectants at a safe distance, have altogether relieved him from the worst of Presidential tribulations. . . . They are the "distinguished men" that make their advent in Springfield for the ostensible purpose of giving their disinterested but unsolicited advice in regard to appointments to the Cabinet and other leading positions, and the policy of the incoming administration. They will first endeavor to hunt him up and besiege him in his downtown office. If unsuccessful there, they will call at his private residence, and, if admission to the Presidential presence be denied to them upon the first application they never fail to make a second, third, etc., one, until their wishes are, *nolens volens,* gratified by the object of their obtrusiveness. Nor are they hardly ever satisfied with the privilege of one interview. They either exact an invitation to call again by conversational tactics or persuade Mr. Lincoln to return their call at their hotels, where once got hold of, he is seldom able to cut himself loose without the loss of several hours' time. It is true Mr. Lincoln's inexhaustible good naturedness is mostly at fault in this. But then common decency should teach the visiting bores of distinction not to improve this excusable shortcoming. Abraham knows that there is no safety for him from this infliction either in his office or in his house and hence he has been looking out for other places of retreat, to which the irrepressible impudence of distinguished strangers would not follow him. Knowing his present anxiety for privacy I would certainly not reveal them, but that the prelude of the Presidential drama, that is, his sojourn in Springfield, is so near its end. One of his secret haunts is the studio of Mr. T. D. Jones, the Cin-

cinnati sculptor, whither he repairs now almost
every morning, not for sittings, but to open and
read his morning mail. The other is the sanctum of
the *Journal* office where he also spends many a
quiet hour.

January 31

Truth can never be too readily told. Why
then the studied attempts of certain parties in
Washington to impress the public with the idea
that the President is not only anxious for, but also
actively engaged in promoting a settlement of the
present misunderstandings between the two sections of the country, by making an epistolatory ap-
peal to his capital friends to accept the border
States' propositions as a basis for such? Why in-
sist upon a misrepresentation of Mr. Lincoln's
views in the face of authoritative disavowals of the
imputed motives and actions? For the sake of
removing a false impression that seems to prevail
to a great extent in the political circles of the East,
I will say again that the President-elect is firmly,
squarely and immovably set against any compromise proposition that will involve a sacrifice of
Republican principles, and that even the proposed

Convention of Commissioners, upon the suggestion of the Virginia Legislature, previous to his inauguration, is looked upon unfavorably by him. He desires to see the somewhat uncertain disposition of the border slave States yield to the rights of the majority, and obedience to the Federal Constitution and laws fully decided by his inauguration, before his friends shall make any move for reconciliation upon the basis of congressional enactments or constitutional amendments.

Springfield, February 3

Will you believe it?—Your most humble representative has been denounced to the President-elect as one of the main instruments of a conspiracy concocted to run Cameron off the track to the Cabinet; one of a "vile band of corruptionists"—to quote the expressive language of one of your Washington correspondents—combined for the purpose of defaming and defeating the illustrious impresario of Pennsylvania. The announcement may sound strange, but it is nevertheless based upon facts. During the last fortnight several bills of indictment have been received by Mr. Lincoln, consisting of copious clippings from the *Herald* and lengthy revelations as to the alleged anti-Cameron plot.

February 4

Cabinet negotiations have been altogether suspended for the time being owing to the commencement of the Message. It is evidently the intention of the President-elect to postpone the completion of the Cabinet until after his advent in the Federal Capital. A semi-official hint to this effect, indeed, has been given out. . . . Altogether the newspaper reading public will confidently expect a total subsidence for the next fortnight of the countless rumors bearing upon the Cabinet-making of the great railsplitter.

February 4

There has been no more noted character in Springfield, next to Mr. Lincoln himself, than Colonel E. E. Ellsworth, commander of the celebrated corps of the United States Zouave Cadets, of Chicago. He is now studying law with the law partner of Mr. Lincoln. [*Mr. Herndon took over the law practice of Lincoln, adding it to his own after the election.*] I recently called upon him at his office, and found him engaged in replying to the numerous letters which had accumulated during the last few weeks in which he has been engaged in stumping Illinois for the republican cause. I found the Colonel to be very thoroughly posted on military matters and, in my opinion, his love for the military will override his intention to become a lawyer. [*Not four months later, May 24, 1861, Colonel Elmer E. Ellsworth was murdered by a Confederate sympathizer at Alexandria, Virginia, when the Colonel was seeking to lower a Confederate flag hoisted upon a hotel. His death, one of the first in the war, caused a great sensation and intense bitterness in the North.*]

February 5

Mr. Lincoln has restricted the time for receiving visitors to one and a half hours each day during the remainder of his stay. A last reception will be given tomorrow evening at his private residence.

Horace Greeley returned from the west this morning. This afternoon he was called upon at his hotel by Mr. Lincoln. The interview lasted several hours. Greeley urged a strict adherence to an anti-compromise policy and is said to have received gratifying assurances. His opinion as to Cabinet and other appointments was freely solicited and given. He is known to be strongly opposed to Cameron and very much interested in the appointment of Chase and Colfax. Colonel Frémont, he thinks, should have the mission to France. Although just defeated in Albany [*for Senator from New York*] he did not ask anything either for himself or friends. . . . The influx of politicians is so great that a large number are nightly obliged to seek shelter in sleeping cars.

February 7

It is almost impossible to denounce in adequate terms the impudent obtrusiveness with which place hunters still crowd upon the President-elect, in spite of his desire to be let severely alone during the remainder of his stay in Springfield. Men came here this week that should have known better. Indiana and Pennsylvania lived up to their reputations of breeding the most corrupt and rapacious politicians, by sending additional squads of Cameron and Smith emissaries. All these gentlemen doubtless came to the conclusion from their experiences with Mr. Lincoln that it would have been better for them to have stayed at home.

The farewell soiree given by Mr. and Mrs. Lincoln to their friends in this city last evening was the most brilliant affair of the kind witnessed here in many years. Hundreds of well dressed ladies and gentlemen gathered at the Presidential mansion to spend a last evening with their honored hosts. The occasion was a success in every respect, with the exception of a slight jam created by the limited dimensions of the building. Every room both on the first and second floor was densely packed with a fashionable multitude. The President and lady received their guests in the parlor on the first floor. They stood close to each other nearly all the evening in order to facilitate presentations. Mrs. Lincoln's splendid toilette gave satisfactory evidence of extensive purchases during her late visit to New York.

I have just learned of a signal rebuke Mr. Lincoln gave a classical snob who endeavored to impress him with a profound idea of his scholastic attainments during a call by extensive quotations in Latin. Mr. Lincoln allowed him to go on for a while, when at last a lengthy phrase attributed to Julius Caesar, induced him to let off the cutting remark: "My friend, I regret to say that I have to refer your classics to these gentlemen (pointing to other visitors) who, I presume, are better versed in Latin lore than myself."

February 9

The President-elect, having completed the first draft of his inaugural, is now busily engaged in arranging his domestic affairs. He attends to the minute details of the preparations for the impending removal of himself and family with his characteristic dutifulness. The close approach of the departure has rendered him unusually grave and reflective. Parting with this scene of joys and sorrows during the last thirty years and the large circle of old and faithful friends apparently saddens him and directs his thoughts to his cherished past rather than the uncertain future. His interviews with the most intimate of his friends are more frequent and affectionate and visits of strangers are not encouraged, but although more than ordinarily moved with tender feelings he evidently fully realizes the solemnity of the mission on which he is now to enter and is resolved to fulfill it firmly, fearlessly and conscientiously. . . . A member of the Georgia Secession Convention called and had a long talk with Mr. Lincoln yesterday noon. He tried to exact a positive committal on one of the compromise propositions from him [*Lincoln*] but was unsuccessful.

☼ III ☼

The Departure for Washington

February 9

The day fixed upon for the departure of the President-elect to the Federal capital is fast approaching. In three times twenty-four hours more the four years' abstentation from this scene of the greatest part of his life will be entered upon. What events may not this quadrennial be fraught with! A more enviable, but at the same time more delicate and hazardous lot than that accorded to Abraham Lincoln never fell to any member of this nation. The path he is about to walk on may lead to success, glory, immortality, but also to failure, humiliation and curses upon his memory. He may steer clear of the rock of disunion and the shoal of dissension among those that elevated him to the office he is about to assume, and safely conduct the Ship of State from amidst the turbulence of fanaticism and lawlessness to the port of peace and reunion. But he may, on the other hand, take his place at the helm of the craft only to sink with it. Why, then, should it be a matter of surprise that the countenance of the President-elect has begun to wear a more sober, solemn expression than heretofore? Why that a certain sadness pervades his conversation and restrains the wonted outbursts of humor? Why that he loves to ·dwell on the cherished past in preference to the contemplation of the uncertain future? Whatever his other characteristics may be, no one that knows him so well as the writer will deny that he has a heart susceptible to all human emotions, and hence is now grieving at the prospect of a speedy separation from the locality that for thirty years has witnessed his woes and joys; that he entered a poor, friendless youth, and is now about leaving as the Chief Magistrate of the nation; that contains nearly all that is dear to him—whose every man, woman and child will see him part with feelings of regret and good wishes for the success of his exalted mission.

Next to the President himself the parties that experience and manifest the most sorrow at his impending departure are our hotel, boarding house, billiard, saloon and rumshop keepers. The climax

of their prosperity is reached. The turning point
of their fortunes is about being passed. As soon as
"Old Abe" will have turned his back to Springfield,
an instantaneous relapse into the former profitless
dullness will come. The quietness of a graveyard
will prevail here after Monday next, and most of
the aforementioned individuals might as well shut
up their establishments and retire from the hope-
less field with what they gouged out of the office-
seekers during the hey-day of "Old Abe's" stay.

It is yet uncertain whether the Presidential
family will accompany its head on his circuitous
journey to Washington. Mr. Lincoln himself is
opposed to their going with him, but desires to be
joined by them in New York. Mrs. Lincoln, however, is anxious to go, and so are many of his and
her friends, and I think it more than probable that
the whole of the family will come along.

Mrs. Lincoln is engaged night and day in per-
fecting the details of the preparations for the removal of the family. She, too, is anything but
rejoicing at the imminent parting with her many
old, tried, faithful friends in this vicinity. Her
impulsive nature will doubtless draw out many a
tear before she will take a last glance at Spring-

field. "Bobby," on the contrary, and the two young sons, are jubilant at the coming good time on the trip to and in Washington. Tonight the Presidential mansion will be abandoned, and the whole party take quarters at the Henry House for the remainder of their stay.

A large number of presents have been received by Mr. Lincoln within the last few days. The more noteworthy among them are a complete suit, manufactured under the auspices of Titsworth & Brothers, of Chicago, and to be worn by his excellency on the 4th of March, and another a one hundred dollar cane from California. The inauguration clothes, after being on exhibition for two days, will be tried on this evening—a most momentous event to be sure. The cane was expressed to Mr. Lincoln without any explanations as to the name of the donor, etc. The oddest of all gifts to the President-elect came to hand, however, in the course of yesterday morning. It was no more nor less than a whistle, made out of a pig's tail. There is no "sell" in this. Your correspondent has seen the tangible refutation of the time-honored saying, "no whistle can be made out of a pig's tail" with his own eyes. The donor of the novel instrument is a prominent

Ohio politician, residing at Columbus, and con-
nected with the State government. Mr. Lincoln
enjoyed the joke hugely. After practicing upon
this masterpiece of human ingenuity for nearly an
hour, this morning, he jocosely remarked, that he
had never suspected, up to this time, that "there
was music in such a thing as that."

On February 11 Henry Villard reported that
Abraham Lincoln "accompanied by his lady and
a number of friends, left his hotel at half past
seven A. M. and rode up to the Great Western
depot." Not until Mr. Villard's memoirs were
written did the fact come out that Lincoln was
delayed in leaving for the train. As the minutes
passed and he did not appear Hermann Kreismann, a German-American politician, was
finally asked to go to Lincoln's room to ascertain
the cause of the delay. He found Lincoln seated
in a chair when he opened the door in response
to Lincoln's: "Come in." Mrs. Lincoln was lying
on the floor, evidently quite beside herself. With
his head bowed and a look of the utmost misery,

Lincoln said: "Kreismann, she will not let me go until I promise her an office for one of her friends." As was usually the case, Lincoln yielded and was then able to leave with his family. At the station there was balm for him: "Over a thousand persons of all classes were assembled in the depot building, and on each side of the festively decorated special train to bid farewell to their honored townsman." As Mr. Villard describes the historic scene portrayed on the stage by Raymond Massey:

The President-elect took his station in the waiting-room, and allowed his friends to pass by him and take his hand for the last time. His face was pale, and quivered with emotion so deep as to render him almost unable to utter a single word. At eight o'clock precisely he was conducted to the cars by Mr. Wood and Mr. Baker of the *Journal*. After exchanging a parting salutation with a lady, he took his stand on the platform, removed his hat, and, asking silence, spoke as follows to the multitude which stood in respectful silence and with their heads uncovered:

"My Friends—No one not in my situation can appreciate my feeling of sadness at this parting. To this place, to the kindness of these people, I owe everything; here I have been a quarter of a century and have passed from a young man to an old man. Here my children have been born and one is buried. I now leave not knowing when or whether I ever may return, to a task before me greater than that which rested on Washington. Without the assistance of that Divine Being who ever attended him I cannot succeed, with this assistance I cannot fail. Trusting in Him who can go with me and remain with you and be everywhere for good, let us confidently hope that all will yet be well. In that same Almighty Being, I place my reliance for support, and I hope you, my friends, will all pray that I may receive that Divine assistance without which I cannot succeed, but with which success is certain. To His care, I am commending you, as I hope, in your prayers you will commend me. I bid you an affectionate farewell."

Toward the conclusion of his remarks, he himself and the audience were moved to tears. His exhortation elicited choked exclamations of "We will do it, we will do it."

As soon as he had entered his car and the train had started Henry Villard went to Lincoln, told him that he had made a wonderfully moving address, that it must be preserved for posterity, and asked that Lincoln write it out so that it could be telegraphed from the next station. Neither he nor Mr. Lincoln knew that there had been a stenographer present, and that his secretary, John Hay, had also made notes of the address. Mr. Lincoln at once complied, wrote the speech out in his own hand and gave the manuscript to Mr. Villard, who, after telegraphing it, treasured the manuscript which he had the misfortune to lose during one of the exigencies of his service in the Civil War. This version of the speech differs only slightly from the accepted one which omits the last sentence. After handing the manuscript to Mr. Villard, Lincoln then entered the private stateroom where he sat alone and depressed until called to address the crowds when the train stopped.

When he wired the President's speech Mr. Villard also telegraphed at eleven-thirty A.M. the following description of the special train:

The train is in the charge of L. Tilton, President, and W. C. Whitney, conductor, and moves at the rate of thirty miles an hour. It is driven by a powerful Rogers locomotive, and consists of baggage, smoking and passenger cars. Refreshments for the thirsty are on board. The cheers are always for Lincoln and the Constitution. The President-elect continues reserved and thoughtful, and sits most of the time alone in the private saloon prepared for his special use. The Yankee Prince of Wales, Bob Lincoln, the heir apparent of the President-elect, adheres closely to the refreshment saloon, the gayest of the gay.

The momentous journey which ended in Ford's Theatre had begun.

The Journey Through Ovations

The progress of Abraham Lincoln to Washington was as if a triumphal journey. Crowds stood by the tracks to wave even when they knew the train was not going to stop. People everywhere turned out to cheer and encourage the man who was on his way to assume the heaviest burdens ever carried by an American. From Henry Villard's almost continuous dispatches dealing with these extraordinary demonstrations and Lincoln's reception of them the following excerpts are taken:

Indianapolis, February 11

The special train reached the Indiana State line at half past twelve o'clock. Thirty-four guns were fired as the train moved in. A committee of

75

the Indiana Legislature was in waiting to welcome the President-elect to their State. General Steele, the chairman, made a short reception speech to which Mr. Lincoln replied. . . . At the junction of the Wabash Valley and Lafayette and Indianapolis roads a large number of prominent Indiana politicians came aboard the train and surrounded the President-elect, who now seemed to have gotten over his parting sadness, and entertained those about him in his usual humorous manner. His hilarity soon extended over the entire company, and wit and laughter became the general order of the hour. A heartier ovation than that rendered him all the way to Indianapolis was never received by any public man. The road was literally lined with male and female humanity. At every station, eager hundreds and thousands raised such an irresistible clamor for a sight of Old Abe as to render it impossible for him to leave their wishes ungratified. He entertained listeners at various points with short speeches slightly flavored with some of his inexhaustible stock of anecdotes. While thus general good feeling and humor was produced by these frequent humorous expressions of the President's, the train steamed rapidly toward this city.

Shortly before five P.M. the suburbs appeared in sight, and a further run of a few minutes brought the train to the foot of the principal street, where a stoppage was made amidst no less than twenty thousand people, and the reception ceremonies entered upon.

The firing of thirty-four guns at Indianapolis announced the approaching train bearing the President-elect and party. The President was received and welcomed by Governor Morton, and escorted to a carriage with four white horses when a procession was formed into a pageant seldom, if ever, witnessed here. The procession was composed of both houses of the Legislature, the public officers, the municipal authorities, military and firemen. Great enthusiasm was manifested along the line of march.

The outside display at this point in honor of the President-elect was respectable, but the indoor arrangements for his comfort and that of his party were sadly deficient. The Bates House is like a bee-hive and standing room can hardly be got anywhere. Only five rooms were provided for the Presidential cortège and they had to submit to doubling up and sleeping three and four in one room. So little attention was paid in the supper room to the President-elect that he was obliged to wait nearly half an hour for his slender share of the repast.

Until this point was reached everything went well and he escaped with comparatively little bodily annoyance, but since the moment of his arrival here he has hardly had a minute of rest. No precautions having been taken to protect him from insolent and rough curiosity, he was almost overwhelmed by merciless throngs before he reached his hotel. He, for a long while, found it impossible to gain an entrance into it so solidly were the stairways blocked up by an immovable humanity, and he only got in by wedging himself through in a determined manner.

Nothing else promising to satisfy the crowd an impromptu reception was opened in the main parlor at seven o'clock. A shake of the President's hand was granted to all who desired to take it. No less than three thousand ladies and gentlemen filed past their Presidential victim. Bob was almost as much annoyed as his father by the persistency with which the curious pointed him out and loudly gave vent to their expressions respecting the "Prince of Rails" [*as he has now been dubbed*].

Indianapolis, February 12

Like the first, the second day of the journey of the President-elect was favored by the most beautiful weather. With daybreak curious groups commenced gathering in front of the hotel and at the time Mr. Lincoln made his appearance every available space in and about the building was as crowded as last night.

Shortly after ten o'clock the cries of the thousands in front of the President's hotel for "Old Abe" became so violent that the object of their curiosity was prevailed upon to come out on the balcony and speak a few words. The President bowed himself into his room, the Prince of Rails was called for and reluctantly induced to appear for the first time in his life before the public. A speech was vehemently demanded, but he confined himself to a graceful waving of his hand.

In the President's room a reception meantime took place. His old Illinois friends, J. K. Dubois and E. K. Peck, took hold of him in a melodramatic manner. They hugged him and told him to behave himself like a good boy in the White House, and lastly even cut a lock of hair off his head with which they rushed triumphantly out of his room.

At half past ten a number of carriages received the President and party and carried them to the Union depot. The train consisted of three passenger cars, one of which was for the exclusive use of the President and suite.

Cincinnati, February 12

All honor to the Queen City of the West. A more magnificent ovation than that extended by her this afternoon was never witnessed west of the Alleghenies. It was not the military pageantry, not the stateliness of civil dignitaries nor any other formal display that made the occasion a perfect success, but the spontaneous turnout of at least a hundred thousand people, comprising all classes, from the rich merchant and manufacturer down to the humblest day laborer to do honor to the man that will be called upon to save the Union by upholding the Federal Constitution and laws.

Columbus, February 13

The magnificent weather today again favored the President's travels. This rendered the trip to Columbus the most pleasant portion of the journey thus far accomplished. The train consisted of three passenger cars in which only about a hundred persons were comfortably distributed. The Presidential family and suite occupied the rear, the local company the middle, and the representatives of the press the front car.

The President, although somewhat stiffened in his limbs by his handshaking exertion last night, and suffering from a cold, was in the best of humor all day, and chatted and laughed continually. Mrs. Lincoln was likewise in her most pleasant mood and conversed with the ladies and gentlemen around her in the most lively manner. Bob did not seem to feel any the worse from the sparkling Catawba with which the Republican youths of Cincinnati had plied him so liberally the previous evening, and contributed much to the general good feeling by his gay, colloquial ways. The two youngest Lincoln sprigs were also exuberant with juvenile delight at the exciting scenes they passed through.

The President was slightly hoarse from his frequent speaking in the open air on the two preceding days and his friends desired him to maintain a strict silence, but his good naturedness made it impossible for him to remain unmoved at the anxiety manifested everywhere to hear and see him. He appeared on the platform and spoke a few kind words at each of the stopping places. Owing to some misunderstanding no provision had been made for dinner on the way; the appearance of two baskets of cakes shortly after twelve o'clock was therefore the signal of great rejoicing among the company. . . .

Verily, the journey of the President-elect is a march of triumph. Columbus is only a second-class city of twenty thousand inhabitants, but its population must have been tripled today. . . . While the procession moved toward the State House with the honored guest of Ohio, such universal, genuine, spontaneous rejoicing as burst forth in every direction at the sight of the choice of the nation for the highest office in the land, proves most irresistibly that the popular mind of this section of the great Buckeye State is fully convinced that Abraham Lincoln will be worthy of the confidence reposed in him, and in the fulfillment of his high mission look only to his country's good. Party distinctions seem to be entirely wiped out among the western masses, the maintenance of the Union, the Constitution and the Federal laws, is the all pervading sentiment to which men of all parties expect the future Chief Magistrate of the country to respond in a truly patriotic manner.

The reception of the President-elect by the general assembly presented a most solemn and touching scene and all that witnessed it felt the deepest emotion. Mr. Lincoln was so profoundly moved as to be hardly able to do himself justice in his reply to the address of the President of the Senate, but the earnestness and conscientiousness that plainly shone on his face effected more with the audience than words could.

Pittsburg, February 14

At half past seven o'clock the special train started [*this morning from Columbus*] amidst the cheers of a few hundred enthusiastic Buckeyes. . . . The train had been in motion but half an hour when rain began to fall first in drops and then in perfect torrents. The President doubtless rejoiced in the weather as it promised to prevent the turn-out of such uncomfortable crowds as had pestered him during the preceding three days.

But the developments of the day showed that

he had vainly expected relief. Nothing daunted by the shower above and the mud beneath, patient throngs had again gathered under umbrellas at all the stations to salute the chief of the nation with songs, cheers, music, flying banners and the roar of artillery.

At the stopping places especially immense multitudes had assembled and brought the object of their curiosity out on the platform of his car by their vehement but good natured clamor. Calls for speeches were universally made, but only reluctantly and scantily responded to. The President's remarks had no particular significance. They were, however, always seasoned with his irrepressible wit and humor, and hence pleased his audiences hugely. The dreariness of the outdoor aspect first spread a shade of melancholy over the Presidential party, but they soon sought to forget the outside gloominess by indulging in divers hilarious pastimes. In the front car the younger members of the company amused themselves in their own way. Speeches and songs whiled away the time. Colonel Lamon treated the crowd to a succession of songs. Bob, whose heart was heavy early in the morning with the remembrance of a Columbus beauty, soon joined in the general mirthfulness and then led off.

Pittsburg, February 15

The rain in which the Presidential party entered Pittsburg last night was still pouring down this morning, but the President-elect was nevertheless true to his word, and appeared on the balcony of his hotel at eight thirty A.M. and delivered the address, promised the previous evening, to a multitude of five thousand people, under an ocean of umbrellas. After the delivery of the speech immediate arrangements were made for leaving the hotel. In spite of the unfavorable weather the streets through which the procession passed was lined on each side by cheering Republicans. At the depot the President was again subject to uncomfortable crowding by the absence of all police force and the inefficiency of his military guard, but he stood in rain for a long while and endured the pressure of the curious without any signs of impatience.

Many interesting incidents occurred. While the party was waiting for the train a little boy was reached over to the President by his father and heartily kissed. Three lassies also made their way to him and received the same salutation. Some members of the cortège tried to take the same privilege, but were indignantly repulsed amidst the laughter of the spectators.

Cleveland, February 15

The train from Pittsburg moved at ten o'clock and had to make its slow way for over a mile through continuing masses of shouting humanity. Six stoppages were made between Allegheny City and this point. The road traversed strongly Republican sections and hence large crowds were met at all the stopping places, especially in the Western Reserve; Mr. Lincoln having contracted a bad cold spoke but little.

As the train approached Cleveland the turnout of the people along the road grew more numerous. The train was stopped at a depot some two miles from the center of the city. Myriads of human beings consisting of soldiers, firemen and citizens generally, on horseback, in carriages and on foot, awaited its arrival. As the President and suite left the cars a universal, deafening shout escaped from tens of thousands. The anxiety to greet Honest Old Abe was evidently intense.

There is but one sentiment among the recipi-

ents of the hospitality of the Forest City; they all
agree that as to splendor of pageantry, kindliness
and heartiness of welcome her inhabitants eclipsed
anything witnessed since the departure from
Springfield. . . . It was an ovation of which Abraham Lincoln could well be proud; nor did he fail
to show deep gratitude and emotion. He stood up
in his carriage and until the hotel was reached
acknowledged the greetings on all sides in his un-
affected hearty manner. The expression of his face
showed plainly that he meant much more than he
could convey by bowing and waving his hat.

Buffalo, February 16

The Presidential party left Cleveland at nine
A.M. today. . . . At Girard several baskets of
splendid fruit were presented to the Presidential
family. No little sensation was produced at this
point by the unexpected appearance on the train
of Horace Greeley, equipped with a valise and his
well known red and blue blanket. He was at once
conducted into the car of the President-elect, who
came forward to greet him. He got off again at
Erie after traveling about twenty miles with the
company.

At the North East Station Mr. Lincoln took occasion to state that during the campaign he had received a letter from a young girl of this place [*Erie*] in which he was kindly admonished to do certain things, and among others to let his whiskers grow, and that, as he had acted on that piece of advice he would now be glad to welcome his fair correspondent if she was among the crowd. In response to the call a lassie made her way through the crowd, was helped to the platform and kissed by the President.

On arriving at Buffalo Mr. Lincoln was met at the door of the car by a deputation of citizens headed by Millard Fillmore [*the ex-President of the United States*]. . . .

The reception in this place was the most ill conducted affair witnessed since the departure from Springfield. A thick crowd had been allowed to await the arrival of the train in the depot so that but a narrow passage could be kept open for the few soldiers and policemen detailed to protect the President-elect. He had hardly left his car and, after heartily shaking hands with Mr. Millard Fillmore, made a few steps toward the door when the crowd made a rush, and overpowering the guard pressed upon him and party with a perfect furor. A scene of the wildest confusion ensued. To and fro the ruffians swayed and cries of distress were heard on all sides. The pressure was so great that it is really a wonder that many were not crushed and trampled to death. As it was Major [*David*] Hunter of the President's escort alone suffered a bodily injury by having his arm dislocated. The President-elect was safely got out of the depot only by the desperate efforts of those immediately around him. His party had to struggle with might and main for their lives and after fighting their way to the open found some of the carriages already occupied so that not a few had to make for the hotel on foot as best they could. The hotel doors were likewise blockaded by immovable thousands and they had to undergo another tremendous squeeze to get in.

Speaking at the American Hotel in reply to an address of welcome by Mayor Bemis, Mr. Lincoln said:

"Had the election fallen to any other of the distinguished candidates instead of myself it would have been proper for all citizens to have greeted him as you now greet me. It is evidence of the devotion of the whole people to the Constitution, the Union and the perpetuity of the liberties of the country. I am unwilling on any occasion that I should be so meanly thought of as to have it supposed for a moment that these demonstrations are tendered to me personally."

Buffalo, Sunday, February 17

Mr. Fillmore called at ten A.M. with a carriage for Mr. Lincoln and both attended divine service at the Unitarian church. Dr. Hosmer, the pastor, invoked the blessings of heaven upon the incoming Administration in a most impressive manner, in his opening prayer. All of the congregation were moved to tears. From the church the ex-President and the President-elect rode back to the hotel and were joined by Mrs. Lincoln when the party was driven to Mr. Fillmore's private residence to partake of a lunch.

Utica, February 18

The train bearing the President-elect left Buffalo at a quarter before six o'clock this morning.

He was accompanied to the depot by Company D
of the Seventy-fourth Regiment. Notwithstanding
the early hour several hundred people were present to bid Mr. Lincoln farewell. The train arrived
at Rochester at eight o'clock. A crowd of people
numbering not less than 8,000 filled the space
around the depot. At Syracuse a crowd estimated
at 10,000 people was assembled to receive Mr. Lincoln. The special train arrived at Utica ahead of
time and was awaited by thousands of people who
were standing in a snowstorm. The Utica reception
was very fine.

The crowds at Little Falls, Fonda and Sche-
nectady were immense in number and very enthusiastic in spirit. At all the stops impertinent
individuals addressed Mr. Lincoln in a very fa-
miliar manner and offered to back him against the
world. He very good-naturedly submitted to the
rough courtesies of the crowd and his remark that
he had the advantage of the crowd as to looks
elicited cheers and laughter.

Albany, February 18

The special train which conveyed the Presidential party arrived at half past two P.M. precisely

upon time, but Company B of the Twenty-fifth Regiment, which was to act as a guard of honor, was very greatly too late. When the train moved up, the engine gaily decorated with flags, the excitement was intense. . . . The police, arriving like the military, behind time, were unable to do anything with the crowds which pressed upon and surged around them. Little boys and big men climbed under and over the train, only to be kicked and thrown back. Ladies essayed to get near the car with no greater success. Mayor Thacher, whom no one seemed to take any particular pride in honoring, was jostled and hustled about as badly as any of them and with the greatest difficulty succeeded in getting a position upon the platform. The Mayor asked if Mr. Lincoln would wait for the military; Mr. Lincoln said he would wait. The wait was a very long one, and afforded a fine opportunity for the display of the relative muscle of the policemen and the crowd. . . . Personal quarrels between policemen and obnoxious individuals relieved the monotony of the general battle, and gave an agreeable variety to the combat. . . . All was confusion, hurry, disorder, mud, riot and discomfort.

At last the soldiers arrived and clubbed muskets soon cleared a way to the carriages and made a space upon the platform large enough to stand upon. Then Mr. Lincoln, who had passed all this time in the car, came upon the platform and was greeted by a faint cheer. A moment and the crowd came forward irresistibly and swept Mr. Lincoln before the Mayor. . . . Standing uncovered even the President-elect was hardly recognized by the crowd, and anxiety to see him and to be certain that they saw the right man overcame any disposition to cheer. When the eyes of the people were so very wide open it is no wonder that their mouths remained shut, and that Mr. Lincoln was not cheered. . . . Lincoln, tired, sunburned, adorned with huge whiskers, looked so unlike the hale, smooth shaven, red-cheeked individual who is represented upon the popular prints and dubbed the "rail-splitter" that it is no wonder that the people did not recognize him until his extreme height distinguished him unmistakably. . . .

The progress of the cortège was uninterrupted by incident. . . . The sidewalks were lined with people, but the crowds were neither so great nor so enthusiastic as at the Prince of Wales's reception.

Not until he turned into State Street did the President have a really hearty cheer. Just at the corner the Young Men's Christian Association displayed the following unique motto: "We will pray for you that you may preserve the Constitution and the laws as they are." While passing this piece of political Christianity the President was loudly cheered, and the shouts continued all the way up State Street, Mr. Lincoln standing upright in his carriage, bowing and swaying like a tall cedar in a storm, for the hill was steep and the carriage rocky.

The Capitoline Park was crammed with people. The soldiery with some difficulty formed a line through the crowd, and Mr. Lincoln passed up to the Capitol steps, the national salute being fired as he entered the building. He was received in the hall of the Capitol by Governor Morgan who addressed him. . . . Mr. Lincoln who appeared pale and wan replied in a low but steady voice. . . . Mr. Lincoln was then escorted by the legislative committee into the Assembly chamber, where the two Houses were in joint session—Speaker Littlejohn occupying the Speaker's desk.

In speaking to the Assembly Mr. Lincoln said:

"It is true that while I hold myself without mock-modesty the humblest of all individuals that have ever been elevated to the Presidency, I have a more difficult task to perform than anyone of them. You have generously tendered me the united support of the great Empire State. For this, in behalf of the nation, in behalf of the present and future of the nation, in behalf of the civil and religious liberties for all time to come, most gratefully do I thank you." . . .

The whole reception has been a sort of failure —a miserable botch, characterized with snobbery throughout. The only part that passed off in any decent manner was the proceedings in the House. The whole affair has opened up developments and heart-burnings that will make hereafter a bitter fight in the Republican party. The Committee fixed upon the Delavan for the ladies' reception. There is no private entrance to the hotel and all the police force in Albany cannot make a passage through the drunken crowd for the ladies to pass. That part of the program is worse than a failure.

Mr. Lincoln's train left Albany on Tuesday, the 19th of February with the President-elect and his party almost exhausted, having been "leveed and receptioned by remorseless ladies and gentlemen. Safe in bed at last, too annoyed and angered to sleep, no wonder Mr. and Mrs. Lincoln departed from Albany with feelings of gratitude for their safe deliverance [*from the hubbub, confusion and the jostling crowds*], and with resolutions never to return thither again."

In the *Herald* of Wednesday, February 20th, the day after the exhausted President-elect's arrival in New York, Henry Villard gave a final picture of Mr. Lincoln as he saw him at that time, beginning with the scene in the private car of the train:

In the special car were Mr. and Mrs. Lincoln and their suite. . . . Martin J. Townsend, Esq., a Chicago delegate, and a great friend of Thurlow Weed, was also on board; but Mr. Lincoln was so unwell and fatigued that he seemed to take very little interest in the political conversation. Mrs. Lincoln chit-chatted with her friends, and seemed all life and enjoyment. . . . It was plain to see that the Lincolns are common sense, homelike folks unused to the glitter and flutter of society. Towering above all, with his face and forehead furrowed by a thousand wrinkles, his hair unkempt, his new whiskers looking as if not yet naturalized, his clothes illy arranged, Mr. Lincoln sat toward the rear of the saloon car.

Putting prejudices a-one-side, no one can see Mr. Lincoln without recognizing in him a man of immense power and force of character and natural talent. He seems so sincere, so conscientious, so earnest, so simple-hearted, that one cannot help liking him and esteeming any disparagement of his abilities or desire to do right as a personal insult. What will he do? all are asking. Mr. Lincoln says that he has not yet determined; he cannot determine until he shall get all possible light upon the subject; but he is sure that he will say nothing "inconsistent with the Constitution"—his favorite phrase. . . .

With the rather argumentative and logical powers; with the intimate knowledge of politics and politicians and with the uncommon homespun common sense which his friends claim for him, Lincoln seems a man to act and decide for himself. . . . He seems tremendously rough and tremendously honest and earnest. Lincoln talks excellently and with ease upon any topic, and tells a story with consummate tact. He seldom tells stories in his public speeches, however. When first in Congress he adopted the hifalutin style, but has since changed this for that Spartan simplicity of manner and diction which all great orators have preferred.

Of late also he tells fewer stories than usual in conversation. As a specimen of what his stories are —and for them he has a great popular reputation— he said one day: "I once knew a good sound churchman, whom we'll call Brown, who was on a committee to erect a bridge over a very dangerous and rapid river. Architect after architect failed, and at last Brown said he had a friend named Jones who had built several bridges and could build this. 'Let's have him in,' said the committee. In came Jones. 'Can you build this bridge, sir?' 'Yes,' replied Jones, 'I could build a bridge to the infernal regions if necessary.' The sober committee was horrified; when Jones retired Brown thought it but fair to defend his friend. 'I know Jones so well,' said he, 'and he is so honest a man and so good an architect, that, if he states soberly and positively that he can build a bridge to Hades—why, I believe it. But I have my doubts about the abutment on the infernal side.'" You should see Lincoln's facial contortions at this point. "So," Lincoln added, "when politicians said they could harmonize the Northern and Southern wings of the Democracy, why, I believed them, but I had my doubts about the abutment on the Southern side."

The story which Lincoln began to tell in Indiana the other day, but which was broken off by the departure of the train, is equally apropos: "There was a man who was to be nominated at a political convention, and hired a horse of a livery-keeper to journey there. The horse was so confoundedly slow, however,"—(here the train moved off amid great laughter, but Lincoln concluded the story at the next station)—"that the man arrived too late, and found his opponent nominated and the convention adjourned. When he arrived home he said to the stable-man, 'This is a fine animal of yours— a fine animal.' 'Do you think so?' 'Certainly, but never sell him to an undertaker.' 'Undertaker? Why not?' 'Because if the horse were hitched to a hearse resurrection day would come before he reached the cemetery.' " "So," concluded the President, "if my journey goes on at this slow rate it will be resurrection day before I reach the capital."

Such are the stories with which Lincoln delights his friends when in the mood, but of late the mood comes seldom.

Mr. Lincoln was not spared on the rest of the trip. He spoke at Troy, at Hudson, at Rhinebeck, at Poughkeepsie, at Fishkill and Peekskill. At every station on the road there were crowds and soldiers, and usually special salutes were fired.

When the Presidential train arrived at New York Henry Villard left it, reported to the *Herald* office and did not accompany Lincoln on the sudden night trip to Washington. Assigned to duty there by the *Herald,* he did not begin work in the capital until February 27.

In 1897, thirty-six years later, after reviewing his Springfield correspondence in preparing his Memoirs, Mr. Villard wrote the following tribute to Lincoln as his matured judgment of the martyred President:

His greatest glory was that his great mission developed faculties, moral and mental, in him equal to its requirements. But it would be doing violence to the actual facts to claim that he was fully qualified to fulfill that mission when he became President and did not require the purifying and elevating influence of the events of the rebellion to fit him fully for his extraordinary task. To illustrate my meaning: When he entered the White House, he was certainly ready, as the record shows, for a compromise on the slavery question and remained so until the next year. He was also a believer in the doctrines of the spoilsmen and practiced them in the distribution of offices. Yet I am convinced that, had he lived long enough, he would have become a sincere and determined civil service reformer. . . . My confidence that I interpreted him correctly remains and cannot be shaken as I confirmed my impressions by several talks with Lamon and one with Herndon.

The Inauguration of

Abraham Lincoln

Henry Villard thus described the inauguration of Lincoln of which he was an eyewitness:*

I saw Mr. Lincoln twice for a few minutes before the inauguration, when, in response to an expression of sympathy with his tribulations [*from the office-seekers, friends who insisted upon consultation, and his efforts to write his inaugural message*] he groaned out: "Yes, it was bad enough in Springfield, but it was child's play compared with this tussle here. I hardly have a chance to eat or sleep. I am fair game for everybody of that hungry lot." His wife again added not least to his worries. She meddled not only with the distribution

* See Memoirs of Henry Villard, Houghton, Mifflin & Company, Boston 1904. Vol. I, pp. 156-158.

of minor offices, but even with the assignment of
places in the Cabinet. Moreover, she allowed herself to be approached, and continuously surrounded by a common set of men and women, who,
through her susceptibility to even the most bare-
faced flattery, easily gained a controlling influence
over her. . . .

Great efforts were made to render the inauguration an imposing occasion. The city itself indi-
cated, by the scantiness of festive array, that the
mass of the inhabitants were hostile to the new rule.
But many thousands, including militia and political
organizations, had come from the North and helped
to give imposing proportions to the traditional procession from the White House to the farther end of
Pennsylvania Avenue. The morning was cloudy
and raw; nevertheless, at least thirty thousand people listened to the reading of the message from the
historical corner of the Capitol. Probably two-
thirds of the immense audience caught every word
of the clear utterance of the new President. Not the
faintest disturbance occurred then or at any time
during the day. On the contrary, the chief figure
of the occasion was lustily cheered. For some reason or other, offensive demonstrations and even

violence to the President had been apprehended, and the small regular force held in readiness for the repression of such attempts. Old General Scott, who rarely left his quarters, owing to his infirmities, made a special effort and was on duty near the Capitol, receiving frequent reports from the army officers in charge of the detachments of regulars distributed over the city; but not the remotest sign of mischief appeared. In the evening, the customary big inauguration ball came off, and, as usual, it was a very crowded, much mixed and, upon the whole, very ordinary affair, though the newspapers the next morning praised it as the most brilliant festivity that had ever taken place in the national capital.

The inaugural message, which its author and those at whose instance it was changed from its original form had expected to act upon the political situation like oil upon a troubled sea, was received with nothing like enthusiasm even by the Republicans, and fell flat as far as the Northern Democrats and Border States were concerned, while the rebellious States spurned it with derisive contempt. This unsatisfactory effect was not surprising. The message was, to characterize it briefly, a heterogeneous compound of assertion, on the one hand, of the duty of the new Federal executive under his oath to obey the Constitution and enforce the laws and preserve the Union; and, on the other, of intimations and assurances that he would avoid action that might lead to a conflict, and that he favored such constitutional amendments as might pacify the South. It deservedly met, therefore, the same fate as the other attempts at conciliation in and out of Congress already referred to. Instead of finding himself relieved, as he had hoped to be, from the necessity of making good his pledges to do his duty against the rebellious States, the President was directly compelled to face that dreaded contingency. It came in the shape of the question of holding or giving up Fort Sumter.

A NOTE ON THE TYPE

The text of this book is set in Caledonia, a new Linotype face designed by W. A. DWIGGINS. *Caledonia belongs to the family of printing types called "modern face" by printers—a term used to mark the change in style of type-letters that occurred about 1800. Caledonia is in the general neighborhood of Scotch Modern in design, but is more freely drawn than that letter.*